The Light Before Christmas

A Musical About the Light of the World

Created by Dave Clark
and Jayme Thompson

lillenaskids

MW00818032

Contents

The Light Before Christmas Intro/Scene 1   5

Decking the Halls   7

Scene 2   13

The Light Before Christmas   15

Scene 3   22

Let There Be Light   23

Scene 4   29

Did the Shepherds Need Shades?   30

Scene 5   38

Walk like a Wise Man   39

Scene 6   45

I Can See the Light   46

Scene 7   54

The Light Before Christmas (Reprise) *with* Joy to the World *and* Go, Tell it on the Mountain   55

Production Notes   63

Cast

BEAKER   Studious / nerdy male

SAVANNAH   Confident, articulate female; a leader

AUSTIN   Outspoken male; a show-off

TODD   Mr. Smartypants; obnoxious but likeable male

JULIE   Sweet female; kind of a teacher's pet

ANNA   Upbeat, enthusiastic female

MR. CUTLER   Adult or older child; could be a male or a female

The Light Before Christmas Intro

Music by
DAVE CLARK *and*
JAYME THOMPSON
Arr. by Dave Clark

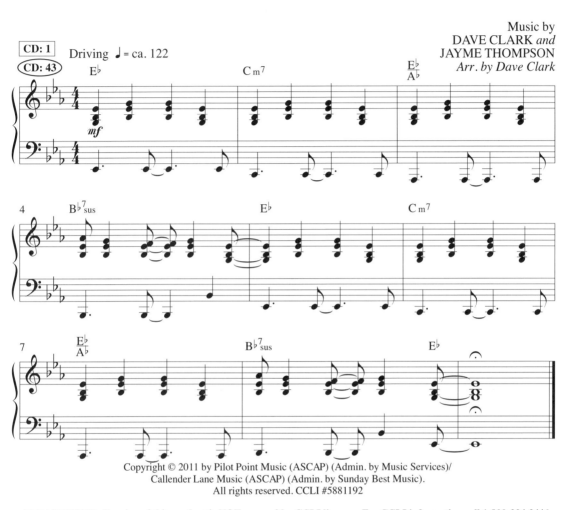

PLEASE NOTE: Copying of this product is NOT covered by CCLI licenses. For CCLI information call 1-800-234-2446.

SCENE 1

(Opening scene is in the science lab and BEAKER *is hard at work adding ingredients to a glass jar. He's the only one in the room and is wearing a white coat and protective glasses. He is reciting each step he performs into a digital recorder.)*

BEAKER: OK . . . let's see. I'm starting with an empty can . . . now adding salt, OK, now let's fill the can with about 2/3 full of crushed ice. OK, now lets take a teaspoon full of water and . . .

(His talking is interrupted by the sound of his classmates entering the classroom. They are carrying a Christmas tree and ornaments and laughing while singing a silly version of "Deck the Halls." BEAKER *is not happy about having his experiment interrupted. When they finally notice him standing there, they seem caught off guard.)*

SAVANNAH: Beaker! What are you doing in here working? Did you forget that today is the party?

AUSTIN: He probably isn't even aware it's December. So tell us Einstein . . . what are you working on today? Analyzing the effect cold has on water? If so, I can save you some time. It's called ice!

(Laughter)

BEAKER: Well, if you really want to know, in preparation for our impending yuletide festivities . . .

TODD *(interrupting)*: Translation . . . our Christmas party . . .

BEAKER: As I was saying . . . I have discovered the formula for manufacturing a reasonable facsimile of simulated snow. It should provide a suitable replication of winter atmospheric conditions.

TODD *(interrupting)*: He's making fake snow as a decoration for our Christmas party.

JULIE: That's great, Beaker. Where did you learn to do that?

BEAKER *(somewhat surprised that someone really cares, he tries to sound a little softer)*: Well . . . it's really not that big a deal. After all, snow is only frozen precipitation in a form of translucent hexagonal ice crystals that fall in soft, white flakes. I just thought it would make it feel more like Christmas in here.

JULIE: Uh . . . yes! That's exactly what I was thinking . . . *(says sarcastically)* translucent hexagonal ice crystals.

SAVANNAH: OK! Enough of this science lecture, we've got a party to get ready for.

(Music begins.)

Decking the Halls

Words and Music by
**DAVE CLARK,
JAYME THOMPSON**
and Traditional
Arr. by Dave Clark

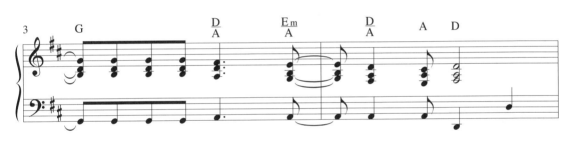

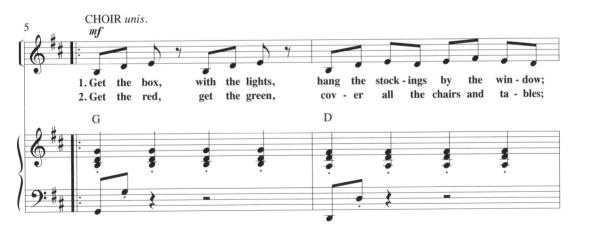

1. Get the box, with the lights, hang the stock-ings by the win-dow;
2. Get the red, get the green, cov-er all the chairs and ta-bles;

Do Not
Photocopy

8

Make a list, check it twice, get the cook-ies, light the can-dles.
Can-dy canes, man-ger scene, gon-na sing some Christ-mas car-ols.

G   D

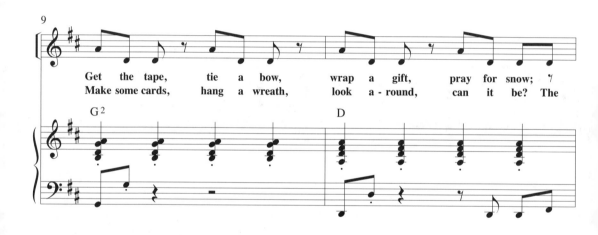

Get the tape, tie a bow, wrap a gift, pray for snow;
Make some cards, hang a wreath, look a-round, can it be? The

G 2   D

CD: 3 *1st time* CD: 45 *1st time*
CD: 5 *2nd time* CD: 47 *2nd time*

Count-ing down the min-utes till we're read-y to go.
on-ly thing that's miss-ing is the star on the tree.

G 2   A sus

cresc.

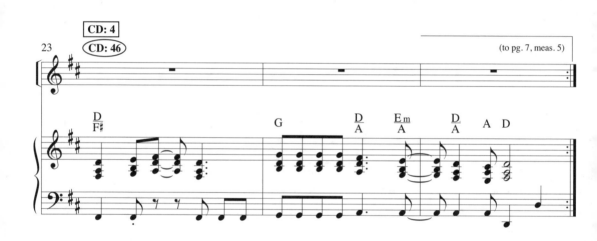

SCENE 2

SAVANNAH *(putting the star on the tree as the song ends)*: There . . . that should just about
do it.

ANNA: I think Mr. Cutler is going to love what we did with his science room.

SAVANNAH: Well . . . he might not exactly love it . . . but I do think he'll be surprised.
I guess we could have at least asked him to help.

JULIE: Are you serious? He would have had us using Bunsen burners for candles and given
us a quiz on cloud patterns and on winter weather.

ANNA: I think he will love it. I mean . . . just look at it . . .

AUSTIN: I'm looking, I'm looking . . . let me get this straight . . . we've got a cardboard
fireplace, a plastic wreath, an artificial tree, and fake snow.

TODD: Yep . . . nothing says real Christmas like fake decorations.

(Laughter)

AUSTIN: Hey speaking of fake snow . . . how we coming over there Beaker? *(Starts to sing, "I'm dreaming of a white Christmas . . . ")*

BEAKER: Almost there . . . the resolution has begun to crystallize and we should be close to . . .

AUSTIN *(interrupting)*: Close to turning on the Christmas lights? Did anyone check them to make sure they still work before we went to all the trouble putting them on the tree?

SAVANNAH: Well, I didn't try them, but I just feel certain they're going to work. Should we wait for Mr. Cutler?

ANNA: No, let's go ahead and do it. Savannah, you get the honors. Can we get a drum roll, please?

(Everyone does a drum roll on their legs and counts down together)

EVERYBODY: 5 - 4 - 3 - 2 - 1!!! *(SAVANNAH plugs it in and nothing happens.)*

SAVANNAH: Oh no . . . this can't be happening!

AUSTIN: Hey Beaker . . . if the North Pole can spare you for a few minutes, we have a bit of a problem over here. Do you know anything about Christmas lights?

BEAKER: Only that they are based on a closed electrical circuit that is connected so that the current passes through each circuit element in turn without branching off.

TODD: No . . . not that! Do you know how to fix them? Everyone knows there's gotta be light before there can be Christmas!

(Music begins.)

The Light Before Christmas

Words and Music by
DAVE CLARK
Arr. by Dave Clark

PLEASE NOTE: Copying of this product is NOT covered by CCLI licenses. For CCLI information call 1-800-234-2446.

12
proph - ets of old;___ They talked a - bout dark - ness and a

B♭sus E♭

14

CD: 9
CD: 51

light that would come,___ For un - to us would be born___

Cm Fm7 E♭/G

16

f %

___ a Son.___ And the light be - fore Christ - mas was the

B♭sus B♭ E♭

f

19

hope of a Sav - ior; More___ than just an or - di - na - ry

Cm7 Fm7 E♭/G

20

He is the light be-fore Christ - mas.

He is the light be - fore Christ - mas.

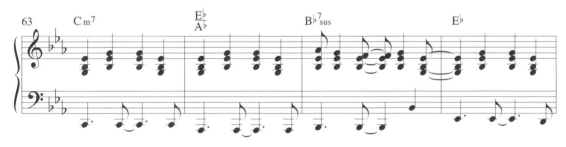

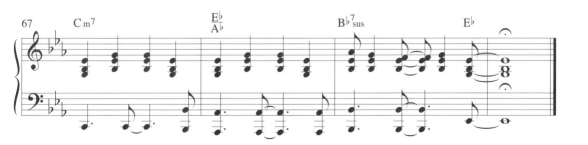

SCENE 3

(MR. CUTLER comes in about halfway through the song but they don't see him. He stands by the door and watches.)

SAVANNAH *(surprised)*: Oh! Mr. Cutler, we didn't see you come in.

MR. CUTLER: It's quite all right. When you asked if you could have a Christmas party in here, I had no idea that you'd go to this much trouble.

ANNA: It really wasn't any trouble . . . well at least not until we found out the lights didn't work.

BEAKER: There . . . that should resolve the situation . . .

(Everyone in the room starts to applaud and cheer for BEAKER as the lights come on.)

AUSTIN: Don't ask him how he fixed it . . . I'm afraid he'll tell us.

(Laughter)

BEAKER: All I did was extract the bulbs and test their resistance.

TODD: I think he means he took them out until he found the bad one.

MR. CUTLER: Well, however you did it Beaker, thank you very much. Hey . . . I know you're getting ready for a party here, but I would sure hate for us to miss out on a chance to learn something as well . . . so . . . does anyone know the story of light?

BEAKER: Are you referring to Isaac Newton's speculation on matter and light?

EVERYBODY *(groaning together)*: BEAKER!!!!!!!!!!

JULIE: If you really want to know where the light began, you can read about it in the first chapter of the Bible. The first thing God did when He got ready to create was to turn on some light.

AUSTIN: That must have been a pretty big light switch.

JULIE: Actually all He had to do was say, "Let there be light"; and there was light.

(Music begins.)

Let There Be Light

Words and Music by
DAVE CLARK and
JAYME THOMPSON
Arr. by Dave Clark

PLEASE NOTE: Copying of this product is NOT covered by CCLI licenses. For CCLI information call 1-800-234-2446.

24

CD: 15 1st time   CD: 57 1st time
CD: 17 2nd time   CD: 59 2nd time

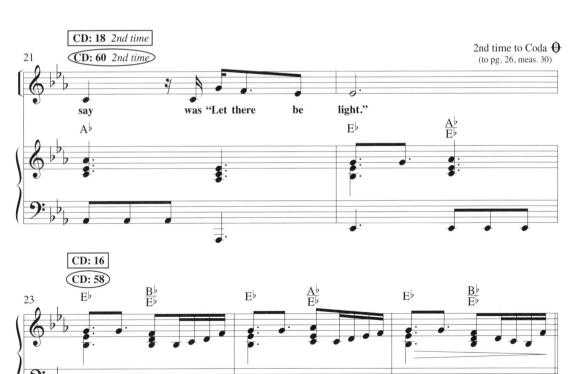

SCENE 4

ANNA: Actually, I think what Mr. Cutler wants to know is the story of light at Christmas . . . you know . . . as in the shepherds on the hillside . . .

MR. CUTLER: Well . . . you're getting closer.

AUSTIN: Closer to this party finally starting?

MR. CUTLER: We've got all afternoon for the party. Let's talk about this for a few minutes. Besides . . . we're still waiting on Beaker to provide us some snow.

TODD: I know there are always shepherd men in the nativity scene but . . . what do they have to do with light?

JULIE: It's more about what light had to do with them.

MR. CUTLER: That's right Julie. It was the middle of the night when the light came to some shepherd men out on the hillside where they were watching their sheep. The Bible says, "an angel of the Lord stood before them, and the glory of the Lord shone around them, and they were terrified." But the angel said, "Do not be afraid; for see-I am bringing you good news of great joy for all the people."

TODD: Translation . . .

BEAKER: I didn't even say anything.

TODD: I know . . . this time I'm the one that needs the translation.

(Music begins.)

SAVANNAH: No wonder the shepherds were scared. If I had seen something like that, I might have done a little dance myself. *(She does a mock dance move acting scared)*

Did the Shepherds Need Shades?

Words and Music by
DAVE CLARK
Arr. by Dave Clark

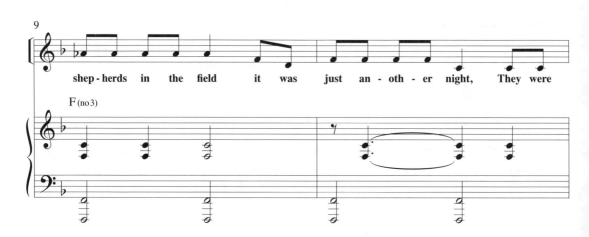

43

don't be a - fraid I'm bring - ing you some great news;

45

Un - to you is born on this ver - y day And you'll

47

find Him in a bed that's filled with hay.____ And

CD: 23
CD: 65

50

sud - den - ly the sky was filled with shouts But there's still one thing that I

D.S. al Coda CODA
(to pg. 32, meas. 23)

CD: 24   CD: 66

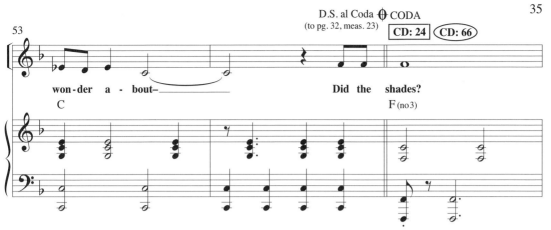

won-der a - bout—   Did the   shades?

CD: 25
CD: 67

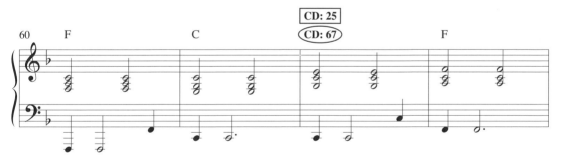

Did the   shep-herds need   shades   in the

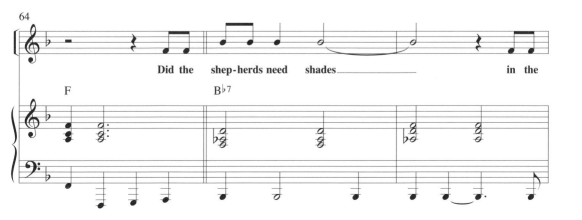

SCENE 5

AUSTIN: So we have the light of creation and the light the shepherds saw. Is this the story of Christmas or the story of light?

JULIE: Well, technically, I suppose it's both. In fact, I think you could even say that Christmas is the story of light.

TODD: As in the lights on the tree?

JULIE: Well . . . not exactly!

TODD: You mean there's more?

AUSTIN: Duh . . . she's talking about the light from the star!

TODD: Any star in particular?

ANNA: The one that led the three wise men from the east to see the Baby Jesus.

BEAKER: When you consider that light travels at 186,000 miles per second, the star you are referring to could have actually been billions of light years away.

TODD: Translation?

BEAKER: Well . . . the star could have actually been in place since the beginning of time.

JULIE: So what you're saying is that God could have known from the time He created the world that He would send His Son to earth?

MR. CUTLER: Absolutely!

(Music begins.)

Walk like a Wise Man

Words and Music by
DAVE CLARK
Arr. by Dave Clark

PLEASE NOTE: Copying of this product is NOT covered by CCLI licenses. For CCLI information call 1-800-234-2446.

13

on - ly thing we've got   is   a   star   to   lead_____ us.

F   B♭   D m

15

We're not gon - na stop   till we   see the ba - by Je - sus_____

E♭   N.C.   E♭

18

Whoa,_____   got - ta walk   like a   wise   man.

D m   E♭   F   B♭

21

2nd time to Coda ⊕   CD: 27
(to pg. 42, meas. 34)   CD: 69

C   B♭   F   B♭   C   B♭

SCENE 6

TODD *(with attitude)*: So God used the light to announce the news to the shepherds and He used the light to lead the wise men to where the baby was and when they got there they found a tree with lights on it and that's why we're having a party!

BEAKER: That would be totally unfeasible since it wasn't until 1882 that the first Christmas tree was lit by electricity. Before that, people glued candles to tree branches with melted wax.

TODD: Where do you learn all this stuff, and why do you feel like you have to share it with us?

SAVANNAH: I think I'm starting to get it. Christmas really is the story of light.

MR. CUTLER: Yes Savannah, it is, but we still haven't answered the most important question.

TODD: Which is, when does the party finally start?

SAVANNAH: What is the true light of Christmas?

MR. CUTLER: That's the question I'm talking about! Does anyone notice anything missing from the story?

(A few seconds of hesitation while they all look at each other. Music begins.)

TODD: I don't think I need Beaker to answer this one . . .

(TODD moves some desks back out of the way, kneels down and motions for SAVANNAH to come kneel beside him. As the other kids catch on to what he's doing, they make a pretend baby out of things lying around the classroom and create a manger scene.)

I Can See the Light

Words and Music by
DAVE CLARK and
JAYME THOMPSON
Arr. by Dave Clark

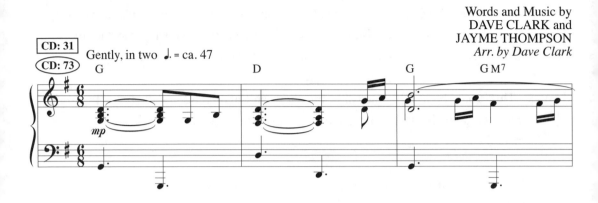

Do Not
Photocopy

PLEASE NOTE: Copying of this product is NOT covered by CCLI licenses. For CCLI information call 1-800-234-2446.

48

25

so long a-go____ When they wrapped ba - by Je - sus in

C   Am   G

27

swad - dl - ing clothes; Tho' I was - n't there still I

C   D   Bm   G

CD: 34
CD: 76
29

know in my heart____ The light can still reach to us

C   Am   G

D.S. al Coda CODA
(to pg. 47, meas. 13)
mf **CD: 35** **CD: 77**
31

right where we are.____ From

C   D   G   G M⁷

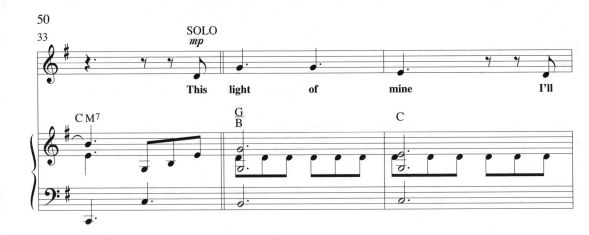

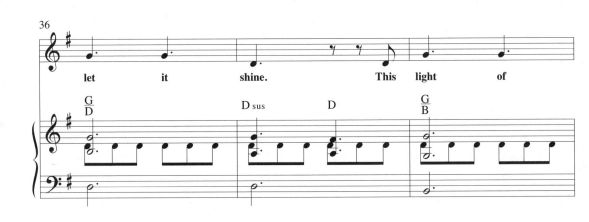

let · · · it · · · shine._____ ALL *mf*

I can see the light._____ From

G/D · · · D

one to an-oth - er, from Je - sus to me____

G · · · G/C

mf

Down thro' the a - ges to this____ Christ - mas Eve;____

G/D · · · Dsus · · · D

53

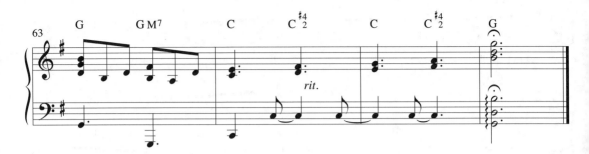

SCENE 7

ANNA: It's Jesus who is the true Light of Christmas.

JULIE: It was His glory the shepherds saw . . .

SAVANNAH: And the star the wise men followed was a reflection of His light . . .

MR. CUTLER: Yes . . . from the very beginning of time, God so loved the world that He knew He would send us His only Son. Long before that night in Bethlehem, God already knew He would send the Light of the World for each of us.

BEAKER: I HAVE IT!!!

AUSTIN: What exactly do you have?

BEAKER: The proper vapor composed primarily of water.

EVERYBODY *(in unison)*: Todd?

TODD *(as* BEAKER *starts throwing fake snow around the room)*: He means let the party begin!

(Music begins.)

The Light Before Christmas Reprise

with
Joy to the World
Go, Tell It on the Mountain

Words and Music by
DAVE CLARK
Arr. by Dave Clark

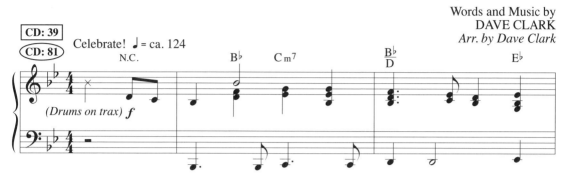

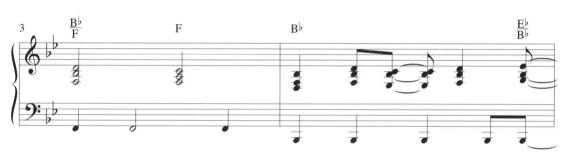

Production Notes

Set Design

The setting is a school classroom. While the demonstration video shows one possible way to set the stage, there is a lot of room for creativity. You'll need a lighted Christmas tree that can be turned on from the stage. The choir could use risers or be clustered into groups. The script places very few demands on the set.

Casting

This musical can accommodate a choir of any size. With a small group, the main characters could make up the choir. With a large choir, the main characters could stay in character during the songs. Speaking parts could be divided and additional solos can be created. The musical can also be performed with no solos.

Special Movement

Movement and ideas for teaching movement can be found on the Demonstration DVD (7-65762-00743-7).

Costuming

Costuming is extremely basic and could be as simple as instructing the children to wear solid tops of red or green. Some costuming ideas can be found on the Demonstration DVD (7-65762-00743-7).

Props

Sunglasses for each child.   Science equipment for BEAKER.